The Christmas Eve Rescue Mission

By

Greg Garson

The Christmas Eve Rescue Mission
Published by CAAB Publishing Ltd
(Reg no 12484492)

C.A.A.B
PUBLISHING

5 Brayford Square, London, UK
www.caabpublishing.co.uk

All text copyright © Greg Garson

All rights reserved. No part of this book may be scanned, uploaded, reproduced, distributed, or transmitted in any form or by any means whatsoever without written permission from the author, except in the case of brief quotations embodied in critical articles and reviews.

This is a work of fiction. Names, characters, business, events and incidents are the products of the authors' imagination. Any resemblance to actual persons, living or dead, or actual events is purely coincidental.

First Published 2025
1 3 5 7 9 10 8 6 4 2
Published in the UK

British Library Cataloguing in Publication data available

The Christmas Eve Rescue Mission

Chapter 1

Mysterious Boxes and the Vanishing Elf

It was the day before Christmas Eve. A crisp Sunday afternoon, after a great day out with their parents, Nathan and Milly were now admiring the Christmas decorations in the large shopfronts of the city. Hands pressing on the glass and mouths wide open, they didn't feel the cold.

"Look at these big penguins," exclaimed Milly, laughing, "they're dancing along to the happy song while the elves are making presents."

"I like the bear ringing the bell, on top of the moving train," said Nathan.

Each shop had its own display, so the children were soaking in all the magic from each window display before moving to the next. Christmas really was a wonderful festive season, and the children enjoyed spending time with their parents at the weekend.

The family walked slowly home, eating warm chestnuts from a street market, and before they realised it, they had arrived at the bottom of the block of flats where they lived. A large delivery van was blocking the entrance, with wooden boxes stacked up at the rear of the van. Milly, the slimmest, managed to squeeze between the wall and the boxes and reached the entrance double doors.

"This is really tight," moaned Nathan, trying to walk past next, pushing the boxes to one side.

"Be careful, kid!" yelled a loud manly voice at the rear of the van. "You nearly knocked these over."

Nathan turned and realised with horror that the loud voice belonged to The Scaretaker, who managed the building where they lived. He was a very imposing character, mid-length dark hair, 6 foot tall and XXL muscular build. A deep, threatening voice, and a prominent scar running from his left eye to his chin, earned the manager the nickname of "Scaretaker", since nobody knew his real name. All the children in the building were afraid of him, as he was always grumpy. He never had a pleasant word for anyone, and today was no exception. He was obviously busy unloading the van full of the mysterious, unlabelled boxes and didn't like the interruption. Still, this was very peculiar on a Sunday.

"Sorry, Sir," said Dad, "but you should clear the access so that people can enter the building!"

"Argh," replied The Scaretaker, calming down, realising that the children were accompanied by grown-ups. "I will move them, but do not touch the boxes."

"He's weirder by the day," mumbled Dad.

"What did you say?" shouted The Scaretaker, furious again.

"I said *Have a good day,*" replied Dad, who didn't want to antagonise him further.

The family smiled and hurried inside the building, away from the irritable character. In the hallway, they met Tommy's dad, so they stopped for a chat. Tommy was Nathan's best friend and lived on the fifth floor. This was the highest floor with opening windows. Above this, it was impossible for safety reasons. So, Nathan often came down from the 23rd floor, where he lived, to play in Tommy's bedroom. They would open the window and throw paper planes as far as they could. If they hit someone, they would dive down on the floor, hiding and laughing until they were in tears. But this was mostly a summer game when there wasn't too much wind. In the autumn, the boys would revert back to their best behaviour, to ensure they would get their most wanted Christmas presents.

"Where is Tommy?" asked Nathan to his dad.

"He was here a minute ago," answered his dad. "We're going to the shop to buy some more mince pies. We're running low, again!" he smiled, rubbing his large tummy with a smile.

"I'm coming!" exclaimed Tommy, showing up from around the corner, walking past The Scaretaker, who was now dragging his boxes across the floor, from the entrance towards the elevator. "I was just looking at a lost elf toy, left on the floor by the lift. But I left it there in case its owners find it when they come back."

"Good idea," said his dad. "Come on, we haven't got long before the shop closes, let's go."

"Goodbye, Nathan, goodbye, everyone," said Tommy, following his dad to the door.

By the time the family walked from the reception, along the corridor to the lifts, The Scaretaker and his boxes had gone. Nathan pressed the call button of the elevator, and they waited patiently except for Milly, who was turning around like a dog chasing its tail.

"Keep still, Milly," said Mummy. "What are you doing?"

"I'm looking for the elf Tommy told us about," replied Milly. "He said it was lying by the lift, but it seems to have disappeared. Very strange!"

"Strange indeed," agreed Daddy, "but the lift is here now, let's go."

The lift took the family up to the 23rd floor, where their small flat was located. The children have lived in this tower their whole life, so it was natural for them, and they didn't mind the city or living in a flat. This was one of hundreds of similar apartments, in this eighty-something storey building, making up the skyscraper towering over

the city. They had a nice family dinner and played a couple of games before bedtime, a weekly treat before their dad returned to work on Mondays.

The next morning, Nathan woke up very sleepy. Once again, he had gone to sleep too late.

Nathan and Milly's mum prepared their breakfast: chocolate rings cereals for Nathan, and honey crunchies for Milly. Milly was very excited this morning. It was Christmas Eve! They had finished school now, and they would have a week off to enjoy late mornings, yummy food and playing with their new toys. It had only been around three years now that Milly fully understood the meaning of Christmas and she remembered the last one as the best day of her life.

"Remember Mummy," she started, "last year Santa brought me my wooden doll's house with the tiny furniture! Perhaps I will get the shop to go with it this year!"

"I don't think you've been good enough," teased Nathan.

"Of course, I've been good, haven't I, Mummy? At least I don't get into trouble at school like you and Tommy," replied Milly, hurt.

Nathan wasn't naughty as such, but he had the habit of chatting and laughing during class. Teachers had to separate the two best friends regularly, sitting them at opposite corners of the classroom.

"Stop squabbling at once," said Mummy. "And remember that we have to go to buy flowers for the Christmas table and a wreath this morning, so please finish your breakfast quickly."

Mummy got the children's clothes out of the wardrobe and laid them on their beds, so that they could get dressed in coordinated outfits. Within half an hour, both children were dressed, combed and wrapped up warm, ready to go out.

The family walked to the next block, where the nicer independent shops were located. As they approached the florist shop, Nathan noticed a familiar van parked on the other side of the road.

"Look, Mummy, isn't that the van we saw yesterday, outside our building?" asked Nathan.

"It does look like it, but there are many vans that look alike, you know," replied Mummy.

"Here he comes," said Milly, pointing her finger towards the van. "The Scaretaker is loading more of those large boxes into the van!"

"I told you it was the same van. What can he be carrying again?" wondered Nathan.

Natural Yarn Importer," read Mummy on the red brick building, as The Scaretaker was going back inside, looking left and right as if to check that nobody was watching him.

"So, this is what he's been bringing into our building," commented Nathan. "What can one do with that much wool?"

"I have no idea," admitted Mummy. "Another eccentricity from our dear building manager!"

They walked past the van unnoticed and continued on their way to the flower shop, which was full of wonderful Christmas decorations. The family walked slowly, commenting on the shiny baubles, wooden ornaments, tissue angels, sparkly stars, and nutcrackers. Further along was a huge selection of wreaths. Some were real, some fake, but all were very tastefully arranged. Milly liked the holly ones, with red berries and a red bow, but Mummy preferred the spruce ones with snowy pinecones. Nathan was looking at the elves, seated on the shelf next to the wreaths.

After a short debate, the girls agreed on a pretty wreath. Milly carried it, and they continued looking at wrapping paper, bags and ribbons. Soon, the Christmas section came to an end, and seasonal flowers filled the rest of the shop. Nathan totally lost interest, but the girls continued to stroll and chose a nice, scented arrangement for the table. Finally, they arrived at the till to pay.

"Good morning, and Merry Christmas," said the florist, warmly. "Did you find everything you were looking for?" she said, scanning the items and dropping them in a paper bag.

"Yes, thank you," said Mummy. "What is this red thing on the wreath?" she asked, pointing towards the rear of the wreath at something unexpected, as the cashier lifted it over the bag.

"What do you mean?" asked the florist, turning the wreath at arm's length.

"There, I can see it," pointed Milly. It's a little Christmas elf, holding onto our wreath!"

"Nathan, did you put it there?" asked Mummy, disapprovingly.

"No, I didn't!" replied Nathan, genuinely offended. "I was looking at them on the shelf over there, next to the wreaths, but I didn't touch them, honestly."

"Ha-ha, they always try to escape!" laughed the florist, embarrassed. "So, you don't want to take it home?"

"No, thank you, we already have one at home!" laughed Mummy back. "We'll just purchase these two things, please."

"I'll have it," exclaimed a loud voice behind the family before the florist could discard the elf on the leftover pile.

They turned and saw The Scaretaker, his arms full of elves already and obviously wanting one more. This was the third time they had seen him in two days, thought Nathan, and that was three times too many! Mummy paid, picked up the paper bag, and they walked towards the exit of the pretty shop. Nathan noticed on the way out that there were no elves left on the shelf. The Scaretaker must have bought them all. He really was a strange character. The children had one last look at the window display, commented some more on the decorations and finally turned around to go home.

Chapter 2

All the Way Down to the Spooky Basement

Once in the flat, Mummy put the shopping away and started to prepare the ingredients for lunch. In the fridge, she found the special milk for reindeers that she had bought the day before, from the Christmas market. She read the label once again, opened the lid, and drank a sip of it.

"Why are you drinking the milk for Rudolph, Mummy?" asked Milly.

"It specifically says *NOT for children*," added Nathan, outraged.

"I am not a child," replied Mummy calmly, with a large smile.

She instantly looked relaxed and rested. The children looked at each other, and Nathan shrugged his shoulders. It was too late anyway: she swallowed a big gulp of the milk. Mummy prepared lunch for the children, singing and cooking very efficiently. She was usually slow and tired after a morning out in town, but she didn't seem to mind today. She cooked the usual pasta and cheese that they all loved, obviously enjoying herself in the kitchen. Nathan and Milly ate happily, pulling the melted cheese with their forks above their heads, laughing. It was a bit of a competition; Nathan obviously was able to pull higher than his younger sister.

"You're cheating!" said Nathan, "you can't kneel up on your chair!"

"Yes, I can, otherwise you're too tall, it's not fair!" replied Milly.

"I can pull higher than you two!" exclaimed Mummy, almost reaching the light over the kitchen table.

Suddenly, the bell rang.

"Who can this be?" asked Milly, while Mummy left the room to answer the door.

"Hello, *Cheeky* Christmas Eve!" declared Tommy, following the children's mum into the kitchen, with a large smile on his face, and holding a remote-controlled car.

"Happy Christmas Eve, Tommy," the children replied, still eating.

"Do you want to come down to play in my bedroom after lunch?" asked Tommy.

"Yes, please," replied Milly quickly.

"He wasn't asking you, Milly," said Nathan.

"Why can't Milly play with you boys? Her friends are away for the holidays, she's a good girl and won't be any trouble," said Mummy, adding a lot more cheese to her plate, to Nathan's astonishment.

"That's fine with me," said Tommy, "we'll just have to share the remote and take it in turns."

"OK, that's fine, but no girly talk!" ordered Nathan, finishing his plate. "Come on, let's go!"

Milly finished her meal as quickly as she could, while Mummy battled with strings of cheese on her chin. Once cleaned up, she rapidly filled the dishwasher, cleared the table and arranged some flowers before starting the hoovering. She was definitely not herself since she drank that milk.

The children cleaned themselves and put their shoes on. Tommy couldn't wait any longer: he placed his car carefully on the floor and switched on the remote. As soon as the flat door opened, he dashed the car through with a buzzing noise. The car disappeared quickly into the corridor, and the children followed swiftly. Their mum was so busy cleaning the whole flat that she didn't notice they were gone.

Nathan pressed the call button for the lift. It wasn't usually busy at this time of the day, however more residents were home due to the Christmas break. They had to wait a few minutes for the lift to come up. Tommy was pressing the remote frantically, jolting the car back and forth, sometimes hitting the wall when he didn't stop in time. Nathan and Milly were waiting patiently, knowing full well that they couldn't expect their turn for a while.

When the lift doors opened, it was almost full of people. The children entered the lift as best they could, forcing people to move back. Tommy drove his car in and parked it between his feet with a bump. Someone pressed a button, and the lift started to go down, which was good since Tommy lived on the fifth floor, well below Nathan's flat. It was a tall tower block, so the lift was moving quite quickly, but had to stop regularly to let people out. As the lift emptied gradually, Tommy started the car again, back and forth. The children were all focusing on the car, oblivious to the other passengers.

The lift continued its descent, until finally reaching a full stop. The doors opened, but nobody came out. Milly looked around and realised that the lift had emptied: the children were the last passengers. Tommy started the car at full speed, out of the lift and into the darkness.

Tommy followed the car, unaware of his surroundings. The siblings rushed behind him and called:

"Wait, Tommy," shouted Nathan, "this isn't the right floor."

The lift doors closed shut behind them, and the lift started going up again.

"Great, where are we?" asked Milly, alarmed.

"I think we went too far down," said Nathan. "This is dark and dusty; I think we're in the basement."

Nathan spotted a glowing switch on the wall, by the side of the lift. He pressed the button, and a faded yellow neon light flickered from the ceiling above them. Cobwebs were shining across the light tube, spiders running away into the shadows.

"Where did Tommy go?" asked Milly.

"Over there, I can just about hear the buzzing sound of his car," said Nathan.

They both followed the noise into the corridors, pressing more light switches as they moved deeper into the basement. Before long, they saw the back of Tommy, who was still running the remote-controlled car until it crashed into a concrete wall in front of them.

"Wait for us!" shouted Nathan.

Tommy turned around, suddenly realising that he had lost his friends for a few minutes.

"This is a great labyrinth!" said Tommy.

"Didn't you notice the darkness?" said Nathan, stunned. "I think this is the basement."

"Yes, you're probably right. I came down here once with my dad to store our old furniture. But this is different. No lockers: this must be a different floor again."

They looked around them and all they could see was heavy machinery, electrical cupboards, cables and pipes running up the walls and across the ceiling.

"We shouldn't be here," whispered Milly, a little bit anxious.

"Perhaps not, but this is really fun!" said Tommy.

"Can you hear a noise?" asked Nathan.

"Which noise? The water pipes or the fans over there?" replied Tommy.

"I think it might be a voice. Be quiet," whispered Nathan.

The three children stopped talking at once and listened intently, with stretched necks as if to be closer to the muffled voice. Sometimes it sounded

calm and sensible, sometimes erratic, and excitable. The children looked at each other silently, and as if in agreement, started to walk very slowly in the direction of the voice, on their tiptoes to be as quiet as possible. Tommy was holding his car in his arms, and Milly was holding firmly to Nathan's hand, as if she was worried about being left behind. The further they walked, the louder the voice could be heard. They reached a brightly lit-up doorway at the end of a long, narrow corridor. They walked even closer, their back against the wall. As they reached the illuminated room, the boys braved a look inside by stretching their heads past the doorframe. Milly stayed against the wall, hiding behind her brother. Agitated shadows could be seen inside the room, with arms being raised and hair being pulled as the voice got louder. The boys ventured a little further into the room, to have a closer look at this mysterious character. Milly followed despite her fear, clinging onto

Nathan's hand, covering her eyes with her other hand. They could now see the back of a man, in dark overalls with tools on his belt, walking back and forth in a state of distress. He was talking to himself, checking pipes and valves that ran along a large wall, and raising his arms above his head in a very dramatic fashion.

"What am I going to do?" said the troubled voice in a relatively high pitch.

"Stay calm, you will find a solution," said the same man sensibly, as if answering himself.

"But there is nobody left! Christmas is ruined!" exclaimed the panicked stranger.

The children were observing all this with their mouths wide open, not knowing what to do next. When all of a sudden, the remote-controlled car dropped on the floor with a crash...

Chapter 3

A Strange Character in Tinkling Dungarees

The mysterious character turned around at once.

"Who are you, what are you doing here?" queried the voice, as agitated as ever.

"Erm, we're just children," said Nathan.

"We live in this building," added Tommy proudly.

"Please don't hurt us!" pleaded Milly, in a tiny trembling voice.

"Hurting you?" wondered the strange man, coming closer to talk to the children. "I've never hurt anyone, certainly not children. But you should not be here!"

As he walked closer, the man lowered his voice, and the children could see his face properly. He actually looked gentle, with a large nose and a thick bushy moustache. His eyebrows were raised high on his forehead, but that was just because he was worried. In the light, they could see he was wearing red dungarees. As he walked, little bells from his belt rang in turn.

"Who are you?" queried Tommy, defiantly.

"Well, if you must know, I'm Mr Key, the engineer maintaining this building. To make sure everything works properly. But you can call me Alan," said the engineer in a much calmer tone.

"Alan Key, the engineer?!" chuckled Tommy, barely hiding his smile behind his hand.

"Yes, I know what you're thinking young man, believe me I've heard all sorts of jokes over the years," replied the engineer, a little bit frustrated. "I always carry fasteners in my belt, and before you ask, I do not have a loose screw!"

All the children laughed openly, looking at each other, while Alan stood in front of them with his hands on his hips. Since he had been pulling on his hair, he looked a little like a dressed-up Albert Einstein. As if to prove his friendliness, he pressed a button on his belt which illuminated the dungarees with little Christmas lights. He was smiling at the children, positively proud of his outfit, chiming ever so slightly as he turned from one child to the next.

"You didn't answer my question," said Alan, in an attempt to stop the laughter at his expense. "What are you three children doing here?"

"We went too far down in the lift," explained Tommy. "We ended up on the wrong floor by accident and used the dark corridors as a challenging maze for my car. Then we heard you talking."

"I didn't want to come, sorry to disturb you, Sir," said Milly.

"Well, I am very busy indeed," said Alan, scratching his head and stopping the lights flashing on his dungarees.

"Doing what?" asked cheeky Tommy.

"Making sure everything is in order for tonight," replied Alan. But he regretted his last words as soon as they came out of his mouth.

"Tonight, is Christmas Eve," said Milly. "Most people have gone home."

"Look, I told you too much already," said the eccentric engineer, embarrassed. "Please leave me alone, I still have a lot to do, and not much time to do it!"

"Can we help you at all?" asked Nathan.

"No, certainly not," replied Alan, waving his finger in the air. "Children must not be involved, certainly not."

"What could be so important on Christmas Eve?" wondered Tommy.

"Everything in the building works fine, you should be with your family and children, getting ready for the big day!"

"The big day precisely," said Alan, getting agitated again. His bells were tinkling fast, to echo his concerns. "This might not be such a great day this year if I cannot fix this…"

"Is this about Santa?" asked Nathan. "Are you helping him on Christmas Eve?"

"Well, you're a very clever young man," said Alan, resigned to tell the truth. "What's your name?"

"I'm Nathan, and this is my little sister Milly. And this is Tommy: my best friend."

"Nice to meet you all. Well, I suppose I will tell you since you've heard so much already. But you must promise not to repeat a word to anyone!" whispered Alan with a dramatic tone, switching his lights on again.

Milly now held both of Nathan's hands, not sure if she wanted to know the big secret which was about to be revealed. Tommy, on the other hand, was beaming with excitement and couldn't wait to hear what the engineer had to say. Nathan was looking at Alan with eyes and mouth wide open, encouragingly.

"How can I start?" mumbled Alan, scratching the back of his head again, walking around in small circles. "I do help Santa, so to speak, with the delivery of presents."

"I knew it!" exclaimed Nathan. "But what are you doing in a basement? Shouldn't you be in the sky?"

"Not at all, children," started the engineer. "How do you think presents are delivered?"

"Santa goes down the chimney, of course," answered Milly confidently.

"And you said you all live in this building?" asked Alan.

"Yes, Milly and I live on the 23rd floor, Tommy lives on the fifth floor," answered Nathan.

"But we don't have a chimney..." announced Tommy, thinking aloud, starting to understand the issue.

"Precisely!" replied Alan. "Not everyone has a chimney, plus it would be extremely time-consuming for Santa to enter every single household, with all the presents, through the chimney! You see, children, as the population grew, and organised itself in large cities, Santa had to become resourceful and find new ways to deliver all his presents in one night only!"

"So how does he do it?" asked Milly.

"Well, what does every single household in the country have?" asked Alan, encouragingly.

"Windows?" tried Tommy.

"Yes, correct," said Alan. "But in tall towers like this one, can you open all the windows?"

"We certainly can't from our apartment," said Nathan.

"Indeed, you cannot!" said Alan. "Imagine if you dropped something through an opened window, it would hurt too much. Fresh air is distributed by the air conditioning system instead."

"Is this where Santa goes through?" asked Tommy, "he crawls through the air conditioning ducts?"

"Oh, dear no!" replied Alan. "This would be even more time consuming. He uses something else that every dwelling has. Think!"

"The door?" asked Nathan, disappointed by the banality of his suggestion.

"YES! For large presents, Santa does enter through the door! Well done!" announced Alan, with a satisfied smile.

The children looked at each other and puffed, extremely disappointed.

"What about for small presents?" continued Nathan, who picked up the nuance.

"As I explained," started the engineer, "Santa has become more and more busy over the years. He cannot possibly deliver all of the presents by himself, and the reindeers are exhausted! So, he now has... shall we say... little helpers, to deliver all the stocking fillers, which are in abundance nowadays!"

"Do the little helpers use the door as well?" enquired Milly.

"Not at all!" declared Alan. "They use a small opening, small enough to go through, which is present in every household, and allows fast delivery of millions of small presents on Christmas night!" declared Alan mysteriously.

"You're pulling our legs!" said Tommy defiantly.

"Not at all," said Alan. "All of these openings are interconnected, like an efficient network of tunnels. They start here for this building, and I control them from over there!" exclaimed Alan triumphantly, showing the wall behind him with both open hands.

All the children could see were grey pipes running from the ceiling down onto the wall, connecting onto some sort of control panel with a multitude of levers and buttons.

"What are you talking about?" asked Nathan.

"This, children, is a wonderful network of tunnels connecting all the flats in the building," said Alan, smiling. "I give you: the toilets and sewer system!"

Chapter 4

Unwrapping the Mystery of Christmas Gifts Delivery

The children looked at each other, puzzled. Has this engineer spent too much time in the basement and gone mad? Certainly, this wasn't part of the traditional Christmas stories you could read about or watch on television...

"Now you are pulling our legs!" exclaimed Nathan after a few minutes of silence.

"I thought you'd say that," answered Alan, the engineer. "But it is absolutely true! In all city buildings, there is an engineer like me to run the system on Christmas Eve! Let me tell you how it all works."

The engineer raised himself up, then started to walk in circles again with his fingers holding his chin. He was mumbling to himself, obviously thinking about how to explain this extraordinary tale.

"Have you ever heard of vacuum transportation?" asked the engineer finally.

The children looked at each other and all shook their heads left to right, in unison.

"Vacuum travel," started Alan, "is a mode of transportation for a capsule within a tube, moving at great speed. You create a tube, perfectly air and watertight. Within the tube, you set a travelling pod, which carries a few passengers. Then you empty the tube of all the air within, to create a vacuum. The pod is propelled, and travels with incredible speed, due to the absence of air resistance."

"Cool," said Tommy with admiration. "But what does this have to do with Christmas?"

"I'm glad you ask!" continued Alan, tinkling. "You see, the sewer system within the building, or in other words, the toilet pipes, is a complex network of vacuum transportation. All the pipes are perfectly sealed, so the water won't leak, and they connect all the flats to this room in the basement."

"But they're full of dirty water!" exclaimed Nathan.

"And the rest!" added Tommy.

"Well," answered Alan, "this is why I'm here. You see, every year on Christmas Eve, I start my most important role of the year. When everybody is asleep, I dress up for the occasion, start the big machine over there, with the large fan and the pipes coming through. Thanks to this control panel along the wall, I manage the water, and the air contained within the pipes. With the press of a few buttons, I empty the pipes of their content, ready for the distribution of presents."

"This doesn't make sense," said Milly. "Toilet's holes are far too small for Santa!"

"Indeed, Santa would not fit in a toilet, let alone in these pipes!" said Alan.

"So, who delivers the presents?" asked Nathan, who wasn't sure whether to believe Alan or not.

"I told you before, children: Santa's little helpers!" declared the engineer, jubilantly and glowing.

"This is nonsense," said Tommy, "nobody would fit in those pipes!"

"On the contrary, children. Santa has many little helpers... usually," said Alan, looking concerned again. "This is my big problem today, children. There are not enough helpers available this year," said Alan, looking very anxious and switching off his lights.

As he finished this dreadful statement, Alan started mumbling to himself again, walking away from the children.

Deep in thought, he seemed to have forgotten that the children were there, and he started playing with the control panel and jibber-jabbering inaudible gibberish. He was pulling levers, lighting various buttons, pushing control switches and raising his arms in the air again.

"Let's go, this man has obviously lost his marbles, the whole story is crazy!" said Nathan.

"Hold on," said Tommy, "I want to hear the end of it. Then we can decide if it's crazy or not!"

Tommy walked towards the engineer, who was still busy with the machine. Milly and Nathan followed, not wishing to be alone. In truth, they also wanted to know the end of the story.

"Alan... Sir?" shouted Tommy.

"Yes?" answered Alan, turning towards the children, as if remembering their presence.

"You didn't finish explaining your problem. Who are the little helpers?" asked Tommy, encouragingly.

"Didn't I?" said Alan, as if coming out of his dreams. "Santa's little helpers are, as everyone knows, elves. In fact, the tiniest elves on earth!"

"Really?" asked Nathan, still sceptical. "Tiny elves do not exist!"

"Of course, they do," said Alan. "As a matter of fact, you probably saw them yourself! Christmas elves are small enough to fit in our travelling pods, dashing through the toilet pipes, which are in fact called V.E.T.S. This stands for: Vacuum Elf Transportation System, but most of the elves call it "the Elf-evator". The elves are great pilots in the Elfevator and excellent at delivering all the stocking fillers that Santa doesn't have time to bring."

"Christmas elves can't drive, they're not alive!" said Milly, dismissively.

"On the contrary, they're full of energy! But most of the time, when humans lay their eyes on them, they freeze!" explained Alan with enthusiasm. "On Christmas Eve, they are extremely busy delivering all the small presents. Once they arrive in the correct household, they open the capsule, jump out of the toilet, find the Christmas tree and leave the stocking fillers underneath. Then they return to the toilet bowl, jump into the pod and return to the basement for the next delivery. Nine out of ten times…"

"Nine out of ten times," repeated Milly. "What happens on the tenth time?"

"They get caught," answered Alan, serious and deflated. "When humans are awake and walk into the room during a delivery, the elves have to stop their mission and play dead. Sometimes humans don't notice the elves, so they continue their mission and return to their capsule. But if they get picked up, they have no choice but to act as toys!"

"So that's why they keep moving!" exclaimed Tommy.

"They are alive!" continued Milly, amazed.

"Sure, they're alive!" replied Alan. "But they have all disappeared, unfortunately!"

"This is unbelievable," said Nathan, "but it's all starting to make sense…"

"What do you mean disappeared?" asked Milly.

"I think they all got caught by humans and didn't manage to come back which is strange. There are normally more than enough for every household."

"I've got one in my flat!" exclaimed Tommy.

"We do too!" said Milly. "We could go and get them, if that helps?"

"Thank you, children, that's very kind. And it would help, however, we need many more pilots for tonight!"

"Where can we find more elves?" wondered Milly aloud.

"That's what I've been trying to figure out!" exclaimed Alan, once again worried and agitated.

"My neighbour has two, I think," said Tommy. "Perhaps somebody collects them."

"Yes, but who? We don't have much time to find out," muttered Alan.

The engineer was turning in circles again, raising his arms in despair. The children were talking between themselves, thinking aloud about how to help with this Christmas conundrum. Milly was still trying to get her head around the whole concept. She loved the elf her mum displayed for the last two years, in various places of the flat. It always posed differently, sometimes resting, sometimes doing something naughty, like riding a reindeer ornament or hiding in the tree. She has always assumed her mum was moving the elf every day, to make the children laugh. Probably Mum thought the children made the elf move since the truth was far more marvellous: the elf had a life of its own and was very active indeed, once nobody was looking! Perhaps it was trying to escape, or just stretching its legs...

"I saw an elf lying in the hallway last week," mentioned Nathan. "I told my dad, who was chatting with the postman, but when we finally turned around, it wasn't there anymore."

"And Tommy told us he saw one yesterday by the lift," commented Milly. "But when we got there, it was gone: its owner must have picked it up, but we didn't see anyone."

"In the hallway and in the corridors, by the lift, you said," mumbled the engineer. "Someone must have picked them up indeed, but not necessarily their owners!" exclaimed Alan with a spark in his eye.

"Who could have them, and where?" wondered Milly.

The three children looked at each other, then turned to Alan impatiently.

"The caretaker must have taken them!" concluded Alan triumphantly with his finger pointing up to the ceiling.

The children froze in horror and exclaimed all at once: "The Scaretaker!"

Chapter 5

A Close Encounter with The Scaretaker

It all made sense now. The children did see The Scaretaker dragging his boxes from the entrance to the lifts, between the time Tommy saw the elf and the moment the family called the lift. The Scaretaker must have picked the elf up on the way. They would never have imagined he was interested in toys, but then they did spot him buying some more in town, in the florist shop. Perhaps he was the collector and kept them all for himself after all! Nevertheless, they had to recover the few which were genuinely lost, at least.

"Indeed, The Scaretaker," said Alan, the engineer. "I don't suppose he will help us and give the lost elves back…"

"Why do you think The Scaretaker is so mean?" asked Milly.

"I was actually in school with him, once upon a time," answered Alan. "We were only kids back then. I used to play football with my friends in the playground, at break times. But young Scaretaker wasn't interested in sport, or friends. He had only eyes for animals: birds, insects, millipedes, amphibians, reptiles... He used to shout at us if ever the ball did land near one of his beloved creatures."

"What was his name back then?" asked Nathan, uneasy about the subject.

"I can't remember his real name, but he hated us all. One Monday morning, he came to school with a massive scar on his face. Apparently, he got it from his pet lizard. From that day, everybody mocked him and called him The Scary, because of the scar, and his antisocial behaviour. He was never popular! Once in high school, we went our separate ways, and I didn't hear from The Scary for many years. Until I got this job as an engineer for the building. I recognised him straight away, mainly due to the scar. It turned out that he had worked on various buildings all his life, as a caretaker. And it seems that over the years, he earned the nickname of Scaretaker, which is very appropriate!"

The children shivered at the story. None of them wanted to confront The Scaretaker about the lost elves, or anything else for that matter.

"Will you talk to The Scaretaker, Alan, about the elves found in corridors?" asked Nathan.

"He hates me because he remembers our gloomy school days and arguments in the playground. He didn't like the nickname either...," said Alan. "He won't listen to me, it's hopeless, children."

"Perhaps he will listen to us?" wondered Tommy.

"Well, his job is to serve the building occupants. But I can't possibly ask you to do that, he's too bad-tempered!" replied Alan.

"Well, we did offer to help," said Nathan. "We can try…" he added unassured.

"Thank you," said Alan, "but be careful! The manager's office is on the ground floor, by the reception. With any luck, The Scaretaker will be there. Good luck!"

Alan walked the children back to the lift and wished them good luck again. Nathan, Milly and Tommy pressed the GF button on the lift control panel and left the basement to find The Scaretaker. Once arriving on the ground floor, they found their way back to the entrance, with the empty walnut reception desk. There was a little bell on display, with a note "ring for assistance". Nobody ever rang, and no one ever helped. The children walked straight around the counter, to the rear of the reception desk, where The Scaretaker's office was located.

The boys took a deep breath and knocked on the door together, as firmly as they could. The children waited a minute or so, but nothing happened.

"Try again," said Milly.

"You try," said Nathan, knowing full well that his little sister was too scared.

"I'll do it," said Tommy, knocking on the door forcefully.

They waited another minute, without result. After a while, he tried the door handle, just in case. The door opened: it wasn't locked! The children looked at each other and braved a look inside. There wasn't anybody in the office, and not a Christmas decoration in sight either. The boys stepped in to make sure and perhaps find a clue as to where the lost elves were being kept. As they walked inside the office, a shuffling noise occurred, as if leaves were being crushed and displaced under foot. They looked in the direction of the noise and saw a large glass tank on a wooden cabinet, behind the manager's desk. The children moved closer, to look at the tank's content.

"I can't see anything," said Milly, moving her head to search between the sparse branches and leaves forming the habitat.

"Look at this," said Nathan, pointing at a jar of mealworms, and a clear box of live crickets.

Tommy took the jar of mealworms, and started shaking it in front of the glass, like maracas. The leaves in the tank moved again, and soon enough, a head could be seen through the branches, with bulging eyes and rough skin. One foot came through the vegetation, then another, and soon a huge, bearded lizard came out of the artificial jungle, attracted by the noise of its favourite food.

"Do not feed him!" shouted a deep voice behind the children.

Nathan, Milly and Tommy turned around and froze, staring at The Scaretaker who had just entered the office. He looked even more angry than usual, with eyes bulging like his pet lizard and a vein throbbing on the right side of his head, opposite to the scar. Even Tommy was afraid and put the jar of mealworms down on the cabinet.

"Sorry," started Tommy, "we just wanted to see what was inside the tank…"

"What are you doing here?" asked The Scaretaker angrily.

"We just needed to talk to you. We knocked on the door and it opened …" explained Nathan.

"Your pet looks fantastic," lied Tommy, in an attempt to calm The Scaretaker down.

"Thank you," said The Scaretaker, breathing normally now. The flattering comment seemed to have worked, and the atmosphere relaxed a little. "But you shouldn't come in here by yourself, and certainly not feed Jimmy in the day! He can get aggressive between mealtimes. He did this to me years ago, you know!" explained The Scaretaker, pointing at the scar on the left side of his face.

"Sorry again," said Milly, looking at the floor to avoid eye contact, or staring at the scar!

"That's OK, as long as you don't come in here again," said The Scaretaker. "Why did you want to see me in the first place?"

"Well, Nathan and I lost our Christmas elves not long ago. We took them to play in the park and must have misplaced them when we stopped by the lift to talk to the mail carrier," lied Tommy. "We were wondering if you found them, by any chance?"

"Both of you! When did this happen?" asked The Scaretaker.

Tommy looked at Nathan, thinking fast to make the lie believable.

"This week, I think," tried Tommy, "perhaps longer…"

"Ah, I may have found them, but I don't remember," lied The Scaretaker.

"Great, could we have them back please?" asked Nathan.

"They are not here. Lost property is kept in the storage room, located on the top floor of the building," said The Scaretaker. "Come back tomorrow, I'll see if I can find them for you."

"Tomorrow! But Christmas Eve is today!" exclaimed Milly.

"I know which day it is, but I'm very busy," replied The Scaretaker, annoyed again.

"Please, we really need them today, before Christmas!" pleaded Nathan.

"You will have to wait until tomorrow, all of you. I'm too busy today to search through the top floor. You should have come to me earlier. Now leave me and Jimmy alone, I have lots to do," said The Scaretaker, showing them the wide-open door.

The children reluctantly walked towards the exit, not wishing to see The Scaretaker getting angrier.

"Is there anything we could do, perhaps search up there ourselves?" tried Tommy one last time.

"Do not make me cross!" replied The Scaretaker. "The lost property room is forbidden to children, and to building occupants in general. It's not a self-service! Now leave if you want me to look for them tonight, and do not come back before tomorrow."

The Scaretaker closed the door behind them hastily, so that they had no choice but to leave the room. So far, the operation was a failure, and they walked back empty-handed to the elevator. The children made their way back down to the basement to announce the bad news to Alan, the engineer.

Chapter 6

The Secret Life of Christmas Elves

"I shouldn't be surprised" said Alan, after the children explained what happened in The Scaretaker's office. "He has always been tricky to deal with and doesn't do any favours to anyone. Still, better you than me trying."

"What are we going to do now?" asked Milly.

"We cannot wait until tomorrow," said Nathan, "Christmas morning without presents isn't an option!"

"The Scaretaker told you that the lost property is kept in the storage room, on the top floor, is that right?" asked Alan.

"Yes, that's right," said Nathan, "but it's probably locked."

"Yes, it must be," mumbled Alan, thinking. "But we might be able to access it, somehow."

"We won't fit through the toilets, if that's what you are thinking!" said Tommy.

"No, of course not, I was thinking about another of your previous answers: the air conditioning ducts."

"Great, let's go!" shouted Tommy, who couldn't wait.

"But they must be all dusty, dirty and... we'll get lost anyway!" exclaimed Milly.

"Not so dusty, the air is constantly flowing," replied Alan. "But I can't possibly let you crawl through there, it's too dangerous..."

"We will be fine!" assured Tommy to Alan. "You could help us, right?"

"Well, I do have the plans of the building. I could direct you from a distance with walkie-talkies," said Alan hesitantly, glad that he wasn't the one taking all the risks.

"Let's go," said Nathan. "But first, let's get the elves waiting in our flats. They could be very helpful, whether we find any others or not."

As Alan was an engineer, he had access to all the drawings of the ducts, archived in a huge locker with multiple drawers. It took a while for him to gather them together, but it was essential to ensure the children wouldn't get lost in the labyrinth of air conditioning tunnels. Then he went with the children to the lift, and they all travelled up to Tommy's flat.

Tommy entered his apartment silently, as if it wasn't his. He didn't want to be caught by his mum, who would quiz him and wonder which naughty scheme he was concocting this time. Even if it wasn't naughty this time, he still couldn't tell her the truth! He looked around in the living room, by the Christmas tree, in the nativity scene, over and under the sofa. Finally, he found a stripy elf with a red and white bonnet, sitting on the windowsill. He was sure the elf had been under the tree this morning...

Tommy put the elf under his jumper and quickly left the flat, without being seen. This was a first! The little group took the elevator again, to the 23rd floor. Milly entered the siblings' flat since she would be less likely than Tommy to attract attention.

"Eh, nice to see you so early," said Mummy, spotting Milly by the front door as she was dusting the ornaments in the hallway. It looked like she hadn't stopped cleaning, the flat smelled nice and fresh!

"I'm just looking for my doll," said Milly, surprised to see her there and active. "I'll go back to play with the boys afterwards," she added, thinking to herself that it was only half a lie.

"OK, make sure you're not late for dinner!" said Mummy, going to the bedroom with the duster, singing Christmas carols.

Milly looked under the Christmas tree for the elf (which was a kind of doll after all) without success. She looked on the chair and under the desk, with no luck. She walked around the room but couldn't see any elf. Milly was about to give up, and returned to the front door, when she spotted the cheeky green elf with long hair lying on the radiator's cover, in the corridor between the living room and the toilet. She had her hands over her head, as if hiding, badly! Perhaps she was trying to reach the toilets, in an attempt to return to the basement, Milly thought. She grabbed the elf by the waist, shouted goodbye to her mum and disappeared into the main corridor without waiting for an answer.

"Well done, Milly," said Nathan, "It took a while, I thought you'd never come out!"

"Mummy saw me and asked me questions...Then I couldn't find the elf, but here she is now," said Milly, handing firmly the floppy green elf. "Let's go up!"

The little group didn't waste any more time and took the lift, up to the penultimate floor, number seventy-nine. This was one of the highest towers in the city. None of the children had ever stepped so high up in the building. In fact, no residents ever went there; it was another technical floor with machinery, only accessed by the maintenance engineers. They walked to a small room behind the lift, led by Alan, who, thankfully, knew his way around. He had removed the bells from his belt to be more discreet. He closed the door behind them and asked the children to hand over their elves. Reluctantly, Tommy and Milly gave their respective elf to Alan, who sat them carefully against the back wall.

"Come on guys," said Alan, "you can wake up, you're safe with us."

The children looked at each other in disbelief. The elves were not moving. Was Alan mad after all?

"Come on, I told the children all about you," continued Alan, encouraging the elves. "We are here to find the others and get on with tonight's big delivery. It's Christmas Eve already, you know, wake up!"

The red and white stripy elf raised his hands to his face slowly, and started to rub his eyes, which, as if by magic, came very much alive. He was flickering his eyelashes, as you do after a long and restful night's sleep and yawned. The children couldn't believe what they were seeing. This little unanimated doll was changing into a little living person, slowly waking up, and soon after getting up without help.

"Hello, children," said the stripy elf joyously after greeting Alan. "My name is Harry. What's yours?"

"He can talk!" exclaimed Milly, smiling and laughing with excitement.

"Of course, I can talk, just as well as you do, little girl," said Harry. "I learn a lot from humans speaking amongst themselves, and from TV! Sometimes I get seated for days in front of your television. I'm not so keen on the news, but I love game shows, if only I could take part one day, win a beach holiday…"

"Ah, sorry, we didn't know elves minded watching the news," said Nathan, apologetic.

"That's OK, we are meant to keep our 'being alive' secret," replied Harry. "But it's nice to be finally introduced. So, what are your names?"

"It's nice to meet you too, I'm Tommy. This is Nathan and Milly, my friends," said Tommy to the elf, almost as excited as Milly.

"Ah, Tommy! I recognise you," said Harry. "You tend to make me pilot your remote-controlled car, whenever I try to escape in the corridor, back to the Christmas tree!"

"Sorry about that," said Tommy, guilty. "If only I knew that you were alive!"

"That's OK, don't worry," said Harry, laughing. "Everybody does it. That's why we have such a great disguise. And I love the car rides they're so much fun!"

"Is it true that you help with delivering the presents on Christmas Eve?" asked Nathan, who liked to check all the facts, especially extraordinary ones.

"It is very true," answered Harry the stripy elf. "I see you met Alan who told you all about us. And this is timid Sally, who is still playing frozen statues. Come on Sally, it's safe to wake up!"

A very shy Sally, the green elf, opened her sleepy eyes. She looked at the children, at Harry and Alan, and finally said 'hello' quietly. Harry gave her a hand, and Sally got up as well, standing behind him for protection. The children greeted her with joy and Sally soon started to relax. She raised her green outfit, to reveal proudly that she was wearing oversized red pants over her tights.

"Did you dress up too quickly this morning?" teased Tommy.

"Not at all!" explained Harry. "Sally wishes to be a Superhero elf. A S-elf, if you like."

In a few swift moves, Sally pulled down her hat that had two holes in front of her eyes and adopted a superhero pose with her hands on her hips, proudly, and no longer shy.

"Now that's impressive!" said Milly excitedly.

"Call me S-elf-y!" said Sally, giving her a high-five.

"So where are the other elves?" asked Harry, "Is it just us this year?"

"I'm afraid so, for the moment," said Alan. "This is why we are all here. We need to find more of you."

"Where are they all gone?" asked Sally. "We are usually two dozen, at least!"

"We think many elves have been misplaced in various places of the building," explained Alan. "The Scaretaker must have collected them and locked them in the lost property room."

The two elves shivered at the mention of The Scaretaker. They had never had to talk to him, of course, but his reputation was fierce. Alan explained the plan to them, and the elves were soon on board to help the children liberate their buddies. Hopefully, their little size would be an advantage, and they obviously knew how to be discreet when they had to be.

Alan unrolled the drawings wide in front of them and found the nearest duct vent with an opening large enough for the children to climb through. They walked underneath. Alan approached a stepladder below the opening and secured it open, before climbing up. Once high enough, Alan unclipped the grilled vent and checked inside the duct with a torch. The duct formed a tunnel from South to North, just as shown on his drawing. He came down the stepladder, gave the torch to the children, as well as a walkie-talkie. He would keep the other one and would stay in this room. Everything was ready for the children to start their precarious journey.

Chapter 7

The Great Expedition through the Building Maze

Tommy went up first, with the walkie-talkie in his pocket. He would communicate with Alan, who would give them directions from below. Milly followed, then the elves, Harry and Sally, who pushed her hat back up. They were too short to climb from the top of the stepladder to the vent, so Nathan pushed them above his shoulders and Tommy pulled them up. Before long, the children were crawling through the duct; meanwhile, the tiny elves could happily walk through without banging their curly hats on the tinned cover.

"Walk straight ahead," directed Alan, "until you reach a branching left and right."

"Are you sure these ducts are strong enough?" asked Tommy, "It's making creaking noises!"

"The ducts should be OK," confirmed Alan. "As long as you didn't have lunch and dinner all at once," he added, mocking the boy.

"That's not very reassuring," said Tommy, who had a big appetite. "This is the branching ahead."

"Then take a right turn, and you should see a rise in the tunnel, at the end. This is where you'll have to climb to the upper top floor."

The children crawled slowly to the end of the tunnel, where they reached a dead end. There was a small vent to the side, where they could see out on the floor below, and the duct continued upwards, like a chimney. The elves climbed on the boys' shoulders, and they started the climb, taking grip on the duct's horizontal ribs at regular intervals. It was like climbing a very

awkward ladder, but they had just about enough grip for their small fingers to pull up.

Once at the top, the duct split into three directions, presumably to blow air into all parts of the floor.

"Where do we need to go now?" asked Nathan.

"Take the left turn, then straight ahead," confirmed Alan at the other end of the walkie-talkie.

The elves climbed down from the boy's back and marched in front of the group. They were enjoying this little trip, having been stuck in a decoration box for a year, or playing dead most of the time. They were now leading the way, excited to be involved in this rescue mission. At each opening vent, they would look through to check if anybody was about. The first and second vents showed large water tanks with multiple pipes in and out. Alan confirmed that they were heading in the right direction.

"Keep going straight ahead," said Alan, "and you will travel over the large central stability room."

"What's the stability room?" asked Milly. "Is this duct going to swing sideways to test our balance?"

"No, of course not! The stability room is below the duct," clarified Alan. "There should be a huge ball, hanging from the roof. It acts as a damper, and swings gently to counteract the wind when it blows on the building façade, to stabilise the building."

"I can see the ball," exclaimed Harry, in front.

"It's massive!" agreed Tommy, as the children grouped behind the elves, peeping through the vent.

"Should there be some ropes attached between the ball and the wall?" asked Nathan.

"It looks like someone is assembling the ropes into a giant braid." commented Tommy.

"There are some more ropes on this long table over there, waiting to be attached," added Nathan.

"That's strange," commented Alan at the other end of the walkie-talkie. "People shouldn't be making things up there. What else can you see?"

"I can see a pizza box and some cans, next to an armchair and a radio," added Milly.

"Look over there, it looks like a home-made wooden box or cage of some sort. Can you read what's on top?" asked Tommy to the others.

"I think it says *gummy*," said Milly, who had excellent eyes. "No, wait, it says "Jimmy!"

"That's the name of The Scaretaker's pet lizard!" exclaimed Nathan.

"And look over here, there is a stock of those large boxes that he was transporting," added Milly.

"Oh dear!" exclaimed Alan. "Sounds like you found the Scaretaker's den! Be careful and continue as quietly as you can. Turn right next, and you should reach the storage room with the lost property inside. The Scaretaker said he had no time to go up, so he shouldn't be around."

The little group continued crawling through the duct, coming closer and closer to their goal. This reminder of The Scaretaker made them feel uneasy, and they couldn't wait to get out. They passed over the large damper ball, hanging from the roof by four thick wired steel cables. The ball itself was about the size of the reception office, and looked as heavy as an elephant, or two. They continued their route, past a partition wall, and travelled over a much smaller room, barely lit. The children gathered around the last vent and looked down silently.

They couldn't believe their eyes. Below them were five elves, sitting in a circle on a central table, playing poker with monopoly money, and another group of eight elves playing "What's the time, Mr Wolf?" Obviously, they were good at freezing! Tommy made a sudden noise trying to unclick the vent panel, and all the elves below froze, suddenly lifeless. Nathan unfolded a small rope ladder, for Harry and Sally to go down. They quickly let themselves down and jumped onto the poker game table.

"Hello, everyone," said Harry. "You can wake up, it's only us, Sally and Harry."

The elves opened their eyes cautiously and felt reassured to see their fellow elves alive.

"How did you get here?", "How did you find us?", "Is it safe for you to be here?" were the type of questions flying from the elves.

"Alan, the engineer, as well as the children Nathan, Milly and Tommy, noticed that some of you were being picked up by The Scaretaker in various places of the building and concluded that you must be stored in the lost property room," explained Harry.

"Stored, you mean kept prisoner!" said one elf, angrily. "We haven't seen a human for months, except that nasty Scaretaker."

"He's forcing us to work for him!" said another, pointing to the other end of the room. "We're making thick ropes from the natural yarn strings that The Scaretaker gives us."

Harry, Sally and the children looked where the elf was pointing. In the darker end of the room, they saw more elves getting busy, working very hard. Some were opening a large wooden box, unveiling and unwrapping a big coil of yarn string. Other elves were pulling many long pieces of string and plaiting them into a thick, long rope, similar to the ones the children saw in the workshop next door.

"And you don't have to work?" asked Harry, turning round to the elves who were playing cards a minute ago.

"We do, but we were having a short break!" exclaimed one. "This can't go on for much longer. The Scaretaker is making us work faster and faster, he's been yelling and bringing more and more string for the last three days. We had enough!"

"Well, it's Christmas Eve already, so we'll need you for tonight's delivery. But tomorrow you can rest. If you're happy to get out of here, then follow us!" said Harry, the leading elf.

With a cheer, all the elves got up, stretched their legs, bent their hips and started climbing the ladder. The working elves dropped their ropes all at once and followed. In total, 26 enthusiastic elves made their way up the ladder and into the duct. They were all chanting and chatting, delighted to be freed.

"This is going to be a long way," explained Sally, "but you must stop talking for a while since we will be walking over The Scaretaker's den."

The mere mention of The Scaretaker was enough to reduce everyone to silence. The children led the way back to the control room through the duct, where Alan was waiting and still giving directions. The herd of elves was following, walking as quietly as possible, some on their tiptoes. They walked past the vent where the damper ball could be seen, as well as The Scaretaker's messy workshop. Nobody really wanted to stop, and they continued their journey through the duct without incident.

Before long, they reached the vertical shaft and used the ladder again to go down. The duct ridges were too spaced out for the elves' tiny bodies, so Tommy held the rope ladder at the top, for the elves to climb down. The ladder was a little too short, so Nathan and Milly helped the elves to step the last metre down.

Feeling safer on the lower floor, they rushed through the last stretch of duct and in no time, met Alan back where they left him. He was very happy to see the children again and couldn't believe being reunited with so many of his dear helpers, who were held captive for so long. They all had a little chatter, congratulating each other for their escape without incident, making sure everybody was alright, then walked back to the service lift. After a short wait, they all squeezed inside the lift and discreetly descended into the basement.

Chapter 8

The Plot Thickens, but Time is Running Out!

"Let's test the pressure system," said Alan, once back in his basement control room. "We have enough elf power to deliver these presents now, but I want to make sure the toilet network and the pressure within it will work perfectly."

Some of the elves chatted away, oblivious to the task ahead and the tests being run. Others, like the children, looked at Alan manoeuvring intently. The engineer was pulling levers, shutting valves, pressing buttons on the controller, checking arrows that were turning to show the amount of pressure building up into the toilet pipes network.

The first quadrant turned red when the arrow approached the maximum pressure. At the same moment, a large clonk to the left resonated, and the pressure dropped off. At the same time, another control panel flashed red, displaying an outline of the tower trembling. Alan groaned a little and repeated the first manoeuvre. A lever was pulled, and the pressure started building up in the pipes...until another clonk was heard to the right. The pressure went down again, and the flashing screen with the tower trembling lit once more.

"What's happening?" asked Nathan.

"I'm afraid there is a problem," replied Alan, looking stressed again.

"The noise didn't seem right," said Milly. "And what is this screen showing?"

"This indicates that there is an issue with the building movements," said Alan. "We didn't feel anything since we are in the basement, but I bet your mum on the 23rd floor felt the building shaking!"

"This is definitely not right," agreed Tommy, "what's causing it?"

"The pressure in different parts of the building, creates stresses in the pipes, and induces movement in the building. Have you ever heard your radiator pipes banging?"

"Yes," said Milly. "Often in the night, and it's a little bit scary."

"This is the same phenomenon, but on a much larger scale! The pipes jerk and clonk all at once, and make the building shake," explained Alan.

"This doesn't normally happen on Christmas Eve," commented Nathan.

"Indeed, this doesn't normally happen," agreed Alan, thinking with his finger placed on his chin, walking in circles again. "The building movements should be counteracted by the tuned mass damper: the large ball you saw on the top floor."

"Oh, I remember the large ball," said Milly, "it looks very heavy."

"But there were several rope cables attached to it, probably hung there by The Scaretaker," remarked Nathan.

"Mmmm... Could it be it?" mumbled Alan, scratching his fluffy hair. "Those rope cables, connecting the damper to the wall, were they very tense?" asked Alan for confirmation.

"It did look pretty tight to me," said Nathan. "Perhaps they are stopping the ball's movements."

"This could be the cause of the damper malfunctioning," said Alan. "And in turn the building would move under the pressure build up."

"What is The Scaretaker doing with these ropes, anyway?" asked Milly.

"I have no idea. Did The Scaretaker say anything?" asked Alan to the elves.

"Not really," replied one. "He's only complaining regularly that they are not tight enough."

"I think he takes them up on the roof," said another elf.

"Mmm, on the roof?" mumbled Alan deep in thought. "I wonder if we could see anything from the CCTV cameras up there." Alan walked to another control panel and switched on a small TV screen.

"I can't see anything so far," commented Tommy, as Alan flicked through various camera angles.

"There, stop!" said Milly, who spotted something on the screen. "Are those ropes between these two walls?"

"Indeed," replied Alan, zooming in where Milly pointed. "It looks like a grillage of ropes, high up in the air. Almost like a net."

"What could The Scaretaker do with these?" wondered Tommy. "And what is

this square underneath, with an S painted on the floor?"

"That's, err..." started Alan, embarrassed. "That's a landing pad, for Santa's sleigh," he finally admitted.

"I knew it!" exclaimed Tommy triumphantly. "Like a helicopter! But with an S instead of a H. Genius!"

"Well, the sleigh doesn't arrive vertically like a helicopter, but a Santa landing spot indeed, to help in guiding him and make sure he finds the building entrance as quickly as possible," explained Alan. "He is very busy, you know!"

"So, the grillage of ropes over it, is a net to trap Santa's sleigh!" exclaimed Nathan.

"Why would The Scaretaker want to capture Santa?" shouted Milly.

"Well, he's crazy..." commented Tommy.

"He hates children, and he hates me," said Alan, deflated, who used to be in school with The Scaretaker. "He probably wants to see me fail and stop the children getting their presents this year. And he certainly holds a grudge against Santa for not getting wild pets when he was a child…"

"We have to stop him!" exclaimed Nathan. "Take down this net on the roof."

"This trap doesn't look complete," remarked Alan. "We could start by getting rid of the ropes in the stability room. This would free up the damper and restore the Elfevator to a functioning state at least. Then The Scaretaker would have no means to complete his net in time, especially without the elves to help him."

"That sounds like a good plan, but when you say '*we*' you mean '*us*', don't you?" commented Nathan, grasping the situation and thinking of the operation ahead.

"Well...if you don't mind?" asked Alan, embarrassed. "I can't do it on my own...please?"

"This is quite risky, it's getting late and The Scaretaker could go upstairs," said Tommy. "If we are caught there, I can't imagine what will happen to us!"

"We'll be imprisoned in the locker room like the elves," whined Milly. "Or worse..."

"Come on," encouraged Nathan, "The Scaretaker said he was busy, so there is plenty of time and Alan will be looking out for us."

After a few more vain protestations, the children made their way up again, with Harry and Sally, who didn't want to miss any of the action. The other elves were too scared to get captured and locked away again in the lost property room, so they stayed in the basement, wishing the others good luck.

The little group took the service lift again to the highest floor, with a torch, walkie-talkies and the rope ladder. The children entered the duct with the two elves, and Alan directed them to the stability room. The children found their way in no time, checked through the air vent that The Scaretaker was absent, and popped the vent grille open. Tommy unfolded the rope ladder, which fell near the floor, in the middle of the Scaretaker's den.

"I will hold the ladder for you up here," said Tommy. "You go down."

"Why us?" asked Milly, who didn't want to go down very much.

"You're not strong enough to hold the ladder, Milly," said Nathan. "Come with me and the elves, it will be quicker if we all go."

Milly reluctantly followed Nathan onto the ladder, with Harry and Sally on their backs. They touched the ground and looked around them. The place was a bit of a mess, with pizza crumbs and empty cups all around the armchair.

The children came near the lizard tank, which looked empty. Jimmy was probably still on the ground floor, with The Scaretaker.

A few metres behind the radio stood the passenger lift shaft, which was merely a steel frame around an opening in the floor. There were no walls at this level to ease moving equipment in and out of the lift car. It looked like The Scaretaker had his own private elevator… the children would have to watch out if anyone was coming up.

A few dust sheets were hanging from the thick cable ropes, being constructed to form the roof trap. These were connected at one end to the damper ball with a turnbuckle, and to the other end via heavy-duty wall bolts and wire tighteners. No wonder the damper ball couldn't move!

"How are we going to do this?" wondered Nathan, looking up at either side of the rope.

"Loosen the turnbuckle by the ball first, which keeps the rope tight," said Tommy, repeating Alan's instructions through the walkie-talkie.

Luckily, Nathan spotted a stepladder, which he moved close to the dust sheets, for Harry and Sally to take down. The elves were very good climbers, so they managed to pull themselves along the rope, detaching the pegs holding the first sheet before moving along towards the next sheet.

In the meantime, Nathan moved the stepladder under the other rope connection and climbed up. He activated one of the two levers with difficulty: nothing happened. He tried the other lever, which loosened the tension in the rope. Relieved, he continued the operation until the rope gave a noticeable bow, to free up the movement of the damper ball.

"Great job!" shouted Tommy. "Start the next rope now!"

Nathan moved the stepladder to the next yarn rope, ready to repeat the same operation. Milly was standing on the first step, to keep the ladder steady. Tommy was watching them both, oblivious to the main passenger lift screen, which was indicating that a car was approaching fast.

Nathan managed to loosen the second rope and went back down the stepladder when the passenger lift pinged. The children looked towards the lift, and The Scaretaker appeared out of the car, looking as angry as ever.

Chapter 9

Scary Confrontation and Wild Chase in the Lair

The Scaretaker was holding his lizard Jimmy on one arm, petting its head with his free hand. It only took him a few seconds to realise that there were intruders in his den. What's more: children! And they were messing with the net ropes. They had to be stopped and punished!

The children froze for a second at the sight of The Scaretaker. They assumed that they were going to be told off. But there was no time for explanations or justifications: The Scaretaker shouted in rage, bent down to drop the lizard on the floor and started to run after Nathan and Milly. The lizard followed, instinctively.

Luckily, The Scaretaker was very big and not very fit, so he wasn't particularly fast. As soon as they realised that they were being chased, the siblings started running in the opposite direction. They dashed under some dust sheets that were still hanging, hoping to disappear from sight. The Scaretaker followed them, dragging his heavy legs as fast as possible.

So far, the elves Harry and Sally had observed the scene from high up on the rope, in disbelief. When the children passed under, they woke up from their stupor and realised they had to help. Sally pulled her hat down and turned into Selfy. As The Scaretaker approached, they rushed to the closest dust sheet and removed the pegs. At once, the large sheet fell on The Scaretaker's head, who continued running a few steps, blinded, before stumbling over and crashing heavily to the floor. He battled his way out of the sheet and finally recovered his sight with a groan. When he managed to haul himself to his feet, the children were nowhere to be seen.

Meanwhile, Tommy described the unexpected events on the walkie-talkie to Alan, feeling very guilty that he didn't see the lift car going up and hadn't warned his friends in time.

"The Scaretaker is chasing Nathan and Milly as we speak," Tommy shouted breathlessly to Alan. "And the lizard is looking up towards the rope and the elves, hissing. It probably thinks they are some kind of prey!"

"This is bad, very bad indeed!" said Alan. "Are all the other ropes down at least?"

"No, there are two left," replied Tommy.

"So, we can't abort the mission, so close to completion..." muttered Alan. "Can you help in any way?"

"Not really," replied Tommy. "I'm still holding on to the ladder for them to escape, especially now that they're being chased! If I go down as well, we'll have nowhere to run for safety."

The Scaretaker didn't notice Tommy, or the elves for that matter. He was looking around for Nathan and Milly, who had disappeared while he was battling with the sheet. He walked around the tuned mass damper, the enormous ball which was hiding the view forward. There was no point running now; he was walking slowly, as silently as possible, listening to the empty space, hoping to hear the children betraying their location. He advanced further within the machine room; it was getting darker and darker. He was looking left and right, between pumprooms, above and below pipes running in all directions.

The lizard was still watching the elves, who were grabbing onto the rope as tight as they could to not fall. The lizard was hissing angrily, waving its tongue in the air, in and out of its mouth rapidly. It was trying to intimidate

Harry and Selfy, and it was working! They played dead for a while, hoping that the lizard would give up. But unlike humans, the lizard wasn't fooled by this trick and had a sixth sense for chasing prey. The elves had to do something soon!

The Scaretaker approached a large tank on legs, high enough to conceal two naughty children underneath. He came down on his knees, then flat on his large stomach to look under the tank. He looked left and right, as far as possible, but couldn't spot anyone in the dark. He started to raise himself back up onto his feet when a metal pipe came crashing down onto his skull. The Scaretaker fell right back on the floor, stunned. Nathan and Milly were looking from above the tank with a smile, satisfied by the throw. Without losing any more time, they rushed towards the opposite end of the tank and came down the ladder to escape

before the giant could realise what happened.

"This lizard isn't going anywhere. It looks hungry," commented Harry.

"Perhaps we could trap it under a dust sheet, like we did with The Scaretaker?" suggested Selfy.

So, Harry and Selfy crawled along the rope, to the largest dust sheet they could see. The lizard followed, keeping its prey in sight, waiting for a mistake leading to one of the elves falling on the ground. Once in position, the elves counted down from three to null and released the pegs: the heavy sheet fell quickly on the floor, over the lizard's entire body. Harry jumped from the rope onto the lizard's back, hoping it would neutralise it. Unfortunately, the lizard was strong, and Harry was way too light! The lizard was shaking angrily under the dust sheet, and started running, dragging the sheet and Harry on its back.

The Scaretaker didn't take long to recover from the hit. He shook his head producing a cloud of dust from the dirty pipe and stood up, determined to catch the children. He heard some running steps behind the damper ball and started to run in the same direction, back towards the den.

"Keep running Milly," pleaded Nathan, looking behind him, worried that The Scaretaker would catch up with them.

"I am," replied Milly. "Let's run around the ball again, perhaps The Scaretaker will get dizzy and give up, like Mummy does on roundabouts."

Meanwhile, the lizard was still running frantically with Harry holding on to the sheet, on its back. It was a mad rodeo, the lizard jumping left and right, unable to see where it was going. Harry was holding on to what he thought was the lizard's neck with one hand and pushing down his hat with the other so it wouldn't fall off. The lizard was getting more and more agitated and sped up all at once. It ran in a straight line, faster than ever. Harry was finding it very hard to stay put and screamed as he realized the inevitable fate: the lizard crashed straight into the armchair, headfirst, body jolting with the shock. The beast stopped abruptly, and Harry got catapulted right up onto the armchair backrest.

The children ran one more lap around the ball. The Scaretaker wasn't in sight, so Nathan decided that they should try to escape and join Tommy back up in the duct. Milly went up the ladder first, with Nathan holding the bottom so it wouldn't move too much. This was a slow climb since Milly was little and not very strong, so struggled to pull herself up, especially after all that running. After what felt like hours, Nathan lifted a foot onto the ladder and started to climb. He heard steps and looked sideways: The Scaretaker was coming fast after him. Milly was safe inside the duct next to Tommy, pleading for her brother to hurry. Nathan accelerated, climbing as fast as he could. He was almost to the top when he felt a large hand grabbing his ankle.

"I've got you!" shouted The Scaretaker, victorious, as Nathan jiggled in an attempt to escape.

"Let me go, please!" begged Nathan, desperate and frightened.

"Certainly not," said The Scaretaker, now pulling on both of Nathan's legs. "You children will pay for disobeying, entering and vandalising someone else's property!"

"Stop right there!" ordered a voice behind them.

The Scaretaker turned around to see who was threatening him. Between the radio and the lift stood Alan, the engineer, holding down, triumphantly, the lizard by its tail, at arm's length. The children were relieved to see him appear out of nowhere, but they didn't feel safe yet.

"Let Jimmy go!" shouted The Scaretaker angrily.

"Not unless you leave the children alone," replied Alan.

"The lizard will bite you, let it go!" bluffed The Scaretaker.

The lizard was now awake and was jiggling wildly to escape. Alan was holding on firmly, but the lizard was getting more and more agitated, increasing its motion. The children were watching the scene intently, desperate to see if The Scaretaker would give in. The lizard was shaking and swinging so hard that Alan loosened his grip on the tail, and the lizard fell to the ground. The Scaretaker chuckled for a second, happy to see that his lizard escaped. However, his face dropped when he realised what was happening next: the lizard started running away from Alan, towards the open lift car.

The Scaretaker ran after his lizard, who entered the lift just as the doors were closing. In the same instant, Selfy pressed down the main light switch. The room fell into darkness, while The Scaretaker was running faster than ever. The children heard The Scaretaker shouting, tripping over one of the ropes and sliding along on the ground at full speed, towards the open lift shaft where his beloved lizard had disappeared. A long falling shout was heard, followed by a loud crashing noise. When the light came back on, Alan looked carefully down the open lift shaft: The Scaretaker was lying on top of the moving lift car, one or two floors down, temporarily stunned.

Chapter 10

Christmas Rescue Mission: Accomplished!

Silence fell, and peace was restored in The Scaretaker's den. Milly and Tommy came down the ladder to have a proper look, Nathan and the elves grouped around Alan, standing by the lift shaft.

"What exactly just happened?" asked Tommy.

"When I realised that you were in difficulty," answered Alan, "I ran up the stairs to help you. I had no plan until I arrived here and fully understood what was happening."

"Thank you for coming!" said Nathan. "The Scaretaker was furious! I can't feel my legs…" he added, massaging his sore ankles where The Scaretaker grabbed him.

"When I saw the lizard lying at the bottom of the armchair, I grabbed it and used it as a bargaining chip," added Alan. "I knew it was The Scaretaker's greatest weakness!"

"It was a good idea," commented Nathan, "until the lizard jiggled and escaped…"

"It worked out in the end, though: the lizard ran away from me, straight into the lift as it was being called downstairs," replied Alan. "The Scaretaker rushed to stop the lizard escaping, but when Sally switched the lights off, he must have tripped and fell onto the roof of the descending lift car."

"I pulled a rope across, while The Scaretaker was grabbing Nathan's legs," shouted Sally the super elf, triumphally. "I attached it to the other wall and that nasty Scaretaker caught his giant feet on it," she added with a smile.

"Well done, Sally!" said Harry, elbowing his buddy, who blushed at the compliment.

"Well done indeed, looks like they are both out of action for a while now," commented Alan.

"What if The Scaretaker wakes up?" asked Milly, still shaken.

"He will be stuck on the lift car until someone calls the lift to this floor," replied Alan. "That is not going to happen on Christmas Eve, no maintenance is planned for tonight."

"We can call the police tomorrow, to set him free," said Nathan. "A night stuck on the lift to cool down will do him good," he added, laughing.

"He will have to explain why he installed an illegal workshop on this floor, let his wild pet run free in the building and tried to stop Santa delivering his presents! Punishing everyone just because he didn't get what he wanted as a child is really malicious," added Tommy.

"This leaves us free tonight to complete our mission," said Alan to the elves. "Come on, let's finish removing the ropes and return to the basement! We'll leave the net on the roof as proof for the police to find. The trap cannot be activated since the net is incomplete, and The Scaretaker is out of action."

Tommy was holding the stepladder this time, and Nathan finished removing the ropes from the ball and the wall. They checked that nothing was left attached to the tuned damper ball, and that it was now free to move.

"Great teamwork, everybody!" said Alan, satisfied with the outcome.

The little group walked happily to the stairs, down to the lower floor, where they reached the service lift. They were all chatting, giving their own account of the events, laughing and relieved that they were all safe and free. The elves declared themselves heroes, Tommy described himself as the orchestra conductor, and Nathan as a marathon athlete. Milly was just happy to be safe and couldn't stop chatting away. Alan was the only one to listen, smiling and nodding to all, in turn.

When they reached the basement, they were met by the other elves and repeated the story once again, which sounded more epic every time. Alan calmed them down and reminded everybody of the important task ahead. The excitement was still intense, and everyone wondered if the Elfevator was going to work this time.

Alan pressurised the system, pressed buttons and pulled levers. Silence fell: the children and the elves were watching intensely, listening for any clang or other noise of disapproval from the Elfevator system. No noise. The pressure kept building, and the control screens turned green one by one.

"Hurray!" shouted Alan.

"We've done it!" continued Tommy, high-fiving Nathan and Milly.

"Well done, everybody, especially you, Harry and Selfy," exclaimed the elves in a commotion.

"The pressure is growing, the pipes are holding, the tuned ball is damping!" exclaimed Alan. "All the lights are green: the system is working perfectly. Let's check the travelling capsules and we'll be ready to go!"

Alan grabbed his bells belt and switched on his dungarees' lights. His Christmas spirit was restored. While singing, he unlocked a large wardrobe and opened the doors wide. Eight shelves were standing, with four ovoid containers on each one. The elves got very excited and started pulling the capsules off the shelves. They inspected them on all sides, checked for scratches, bumps and dents. Harry pressed a button on the side, and the top of the capsule lifted open. He jumped into it and lay in position, visibly comfortable. He was

holding the handles firmly with a big smile on his face. Obviously, he couldn't wait for the delivery to begin!

"It seems that all is in order," declared Alan. "All that is left is gathering the presents, thousands of little stocking fillers to be delivered." Alan's voice turned serious, and he added: "I am very grateful for your help, children, but you cannot see the presents."

"Fair enough," said Nathan. "We don't want to spoil the surprise."

"I don't mind," said Tommy, "let me see!"

"I cannot allow that, I'm afraid," said Alan. "Besides, your parents must be wondering where you are!"

"That is true," said Milly. "Mummy asked us to be back for dinner. She will be worried!"

"All right," conceded Tommy. "I guess we will go now."

"Thank you, but do not underestimate the role you've played tonight, children," said Alan. "The elves and I appreciate enormously what you've done. It's amazing what we can achieve when we work together. It's a great team effort; all of us literally saved Christmas today!"

The children shook Alan's hand, as well as the elves. Sally preferred a hug, so there was a lot of bending and shaking going on, warm embraces and good words being exchanged. The children wished the elves good luck and walked back to the lift, waving goodbye as they left.

The children waited for the lift in silence, reminiscing about the events of the day in their heads. This truly was an incredible Christmas Eve! They would love to tell their friends about it after the holidays, but they were sworn to secrecy. Nobody could know, or some of the magic of Christmas would be spoilt, and the important role the elves played would be compromised forever. The lift went up to the fifth floor, and Tommy waved goodbye to his friends quietly.

At last, on the 23rd floor, Nathan and Milly walked out slowly towards their door, wanting to stay in the moment and dreading the comments from their parents for being so late home. The new wreath was hanging proudly on the door: Santa couldn't miss it! Nathan opened the door silently, and they both came inside, took their shoes off, got comfortable and went to sit down in the kitchen.

"Where have you been, you two?" asked Mummy, rushing to the children, concerned but not cross.

"We were with Tommy, you know," replied Nathan, looking down. "We played in the basement."

"Well, I don't think children are allowed to play in the basement. Next time, come back up, we've been very worried about you. Nobody wants to call the police for missing children on Christmas Eve..." said Mummy, waving her arms in the air.

"Sorry, Mummy," said Milly, hoping that the interrogation was over.

"Well, I'm pleased to see you now. Come and have some dinner, then you can go straight to your bath!" added Mummy.

And so, they went. Nathan and Milly kept on their best behaviour all evening. They ate their dinner quietly, without fighting or mischief. Then they prepared Santa's snack as well as the milk and carrot for Rudolph. Mummy seemed back to normal, but Nathan wasn't going to try the milk: the smell was repulsive.

They played around the Christmas tree and sang some carols with their mum and dad, who had just come home from work. They washed and went to bed, much later than usual, despite being so tired from their adventures. This year, they learned secrets that even their parents didn't know. Seeing the Christmas elves would never be the same, and they would remember this day forever. They did achieve the impossible by teaming up with these tiny but smart creatures.

Hours after Nathan and Milly went to sleep, the elves started to get busy in the basement. They held their position, each and every one of them lying tight in their capsule, full of tiny gifts. They just needed the go-ahead from the big man, and they would be dashing through the pipes, bringing joy and happiness to every household in the building.

THE END.

About the Author

Greg Garson grew up in France and moved to South Wales (UK) after university, where he developed a unique 'Frelsh' accent.

Father to a growing dreamer, Greg's aim is to encourage children to reflect and imagine by incorporating bits of his primary job as a structural engineer into fun and inventive stories.

The Christmas Eve Rescue Mission is Greg's first published book.

Printed in Dunstable, United Kingdom